World's Funniest Jokes for Kids!

Mike Mains

Published by Mystery, Adventure, Detective Books

Copyright © 2022 by Mike Mains

ISBN: 978-1953-006-301 Paperback

ISBN: 978-1953-006-325 Hardback

Author contact mainsmike@yahoo.com

Contents

A Note to the Reader

Do you like to laugh?

Do you like making other people laugh?

If you answered yes to both questions, then this is the book for you. Inside these pages you'll find hundreds of the world's funniest jokes and limericks for kids, each and every one personally tested by yours truly. Most of these jokes are ones you've never heard before. How do I know that? Because I made them up myself!

Did you know that it's impossible to be mad at someone with whom you've just shared a laugh? It's true. Humor is very healing. That's why if you want to make friends, telling someone a joke is a great way to start. People like to be around other people who make them laugh.

One word of advice: never tell a joke that might hurt someone else's feelings.

The purpose of humor is to make people feel better, not worse. So never laugh at a person who falls down or does something stupid. Never laugh at a person who looks funny. A person who looks funny feels bad enough; your laughter will only make them feel worse. Even if you laugh in a good-natured way it can still hurt their feelings.

With fictional characters it's different. We can laugh at the pain of fictional characters, because we recognize ourselves in them and because we know they are not real. When Lucy pulls the football away from Charlie Brown and he goes flying up in the air, we laugh because we ourselves have been fooled so many times.

Are you ready for your first laugh?

Fantastic! Turn the page and let's get started!

World's Funniest Jokes!

How do you make a hot dog stand?

Take away its chair.

What do snowmen eat for breakfast?

Frosted flakes.

What do you call an old snowman?

Water.

Why did the golfer change his socks?

He made a hole in one.

If hot and cold had a race, who would win?

Hot would win, because anyone can catch a cold.

Why are dull pencils like bad jokes?

They have no point.

What type of tree fits in your hand?

A palm tree.

What did the hat say to the scarf?

You hang around, I'll go on ahead.

What do pickles say when they're in a jam?

Dill with it.

How do oceans say hello?

They wave.

What do you call a funny mountain?

Hill-arious.

Why are calendars old-fashioned?

Their days are numbered.

Why did the banana see a doctor?

It wasn't peeling well.

What does a ball of yarn say when it wakes up in the morning?

Rise and twine!

What did the left eye say to the right eye?

Between us, something smells.

How do you keep a person in suspense?

I'll tell you later.

What did one wall say to the other wall?

I'll meet you at the corner.

What did the ceiling say to the floor?

Stop looking at me!

How do you keep your foot from falling asleep?

Wear loud socks.

Why did the tomato turn red?

He saw the salad dressing.

What do you call a fake noodle?

Impasta.

What do lawyers wear to court?

A law suit.

What happened to the wooden car?

It wooden go.

What's the only mountain in the world that has never been climbed?

Mount Neverest.

What do you call a sad space ship?

A crying saucer.

Why was the belt arrested?

It held up a pair of pants.

Why was the baseball player arrested?

He stole second base.

How do you start a fire with two sticks?

Make sure one is a match.

What happens when a red ship crashes into a blue ship?

The sailors get marooned.

Why was the lightning storm sad?

Somebody stole his thunder.

Why was the astronaut hungry?

He missed his launch.

What do you call a crazy astronaut?

An astro-nut.

Why did the clock go on vacation?

It needed to unwind.

What happens when you throw a blue book into the Red Sea?

It gets wet.

Why was the clock bored?

It had too much time on its hands.

What gets wetter the more it dries?

A towel.

Why is 6 afraid of 7?

Because 7, 8, 9.

What can you catch but never throw?

A cold.

Name four days of the week that start with the letter "t".

Tuesday, Thursday, today and tomorrow.

What did one plate say to the other plate?

Dinner is on me.

What kind of fruit grows in volcanoes?

Lava-cados.

What do clouds wear for clothes?

Thunderwear.

How can you tell when a bucket is sick?

It looks pail.

What do you call a period of time when nerds rule the world?

The Dork Ages.

What has four legs but never walks?

A chair.

What goes up and down but never moves?

A flight of stairs.

What do you call a shaky stack of pancakes?

A panquake.

What do you call bread with a bad attitude?

Sourdough.

What did the pencil say to the pencil sharpener?

Stop going around in circles and get to the point.

What time is it when the clock strikes thirteen?

Time to get a new clock.

What stays in the corner, but travels around the world?

A postage stamp.

A voice teacher knocks on the door and tells the woman who answers, "I'm here to give you voice lessons." The woman says, "But I didn't call you." The voice teacher says, "Your neighbors did."

A man answers the phone and says, "Really? You don't say! ... Isn't that amazing? ... You don't say! ... Thanks for calling." He hangs up and his wife looks at him and asks who it was. The man says, "He didn't say."

World's Funniest Boy and Girl Jokes!

Why was the boy suspicious of bushes?

They looked shady.

Why was the girl suspicious of stairs?

She thought they were up to something.

Why did the boy hit his cake with a hammer?

His mother told him it was pound cake.

Why did the girl eat her homework?

Her teacher said it was a piece of cake.

Why did the boy throw his clock out the window?

He wanted to see time fly.

Why did the girl put her money in the freezer?

She wanted cold hard cash.

Why did the boy run in circles around his bed?

He wanted to catch up on his sleep.

Why did the girl put lipstick on her forehead?

She wanted to make up her mind.

Why did the boy wear three socks to school?

His mother told him he'd grown another foot.

Why did the girl eat her crayons?

There were so many broken ones they looked like jelly beans.

Why did the boy hide a clock under his desk.

He wanted to work overtime.

A father tells his son, "When I was your age, I walked five miles to school every day barefoot in the snow." His son says, "I didn't know there were schools in the North Pole."

A mother tells her daughter, "When I was your age, I cleaned my room, made my bed, and walked the dog every morning before school." Her daughter says, "That's nothing. Every morning before school, I charge my phone, check my text messages, and call all of my friends."

World's Funniest School Jokes!

What happens when a hamburger misses school?

It has ketchup time.

What do 1st graders know that 2nd graders don't?

What it's like to be only one year removed from kindergarten.

Why are school lockers like the Bermuda Triangle?

Stuff goes in and never comes out.

What do elves learn in school?

The elf-abet.

What do monkeys learn in school?

Monkey business.

Why was the broom late for school?

It overswept.

Why was the math book sad?

It had too many problems.

Why do school librarians need long ladders?

To reach the tall tales.

What do say when a teacher grades you zero?

"Thanks for nothing."

A teacher tells a boy she is sending him home from school, because he keeps pretending to be a Transformer. The boy says, "No, wait! I can change."

A teacher looks down over her desk at three boys standing in front of her and says to the first boy, "Where's your homework?" The first boy says, "My dog ate it." The teacher says to the second boy, "Where's your homework?" The second boy says, "My cat ate it." The teacher says to the third boy, "Where's *your* homework?" The third boy says, "The rain ate it." The teacher says, "That's impossible! How can the rain eat your homework?" The boy says, "It was raining cats and dogs."

A girl tells her teacher, "I ain't got no pencil." Her teacher corrects her, "I *haven't* got a pencil." The girl says, "What happened to all the pencils?"

A mother asks her daughter what she learned after her first day at school. Her daughter says, "Not much. They want me to come back tomorrow."

A father asks his son what he learned in school that day. The boy replies, "I learned that horses eat hay, monkeys eat bananas, and dogs eat homework."

A math teacher says to her class, "Who invented fractions?" A boy answers, "Henry the 1/8th."

A math teacher says to her class, "If you have $10 in your front right pocket, $10 in your front left pocket, and $20 in your back pocket, what do you have?" A boy answers, "Somebody else's pants."

World's Funniest Animal Jokes!

What do you call a duck on the 4th of July?

A fire quacker.

When do ducks wake up?

At the quack of dawn.

What do you call a smart duck?

A wise-quacker.

Who's smarter than a talking parrot?

A spelling bee.

What do you call a duck riding on the back of a cow?

Milk and quackers.

Why do ducks make good detectives?

They know how to quack the case.

What do you call a duck that wins the lottery?

A lucky ducky.

Why did the elephant sell his car?

He didn't like the trunk.

How do you know when an elephant is under your bed?

Your head hits the ceiling.

How do you know when a monkey is under your bed?

You step out of bed and slip on a banana peel.

How do you know when a lion is under your bed?

You hear a hungry growl and run for your life.

If a porcupine and a dictionary had an argument, who would win?

The dictionary would win, because while the porcupine has a lot of good points, the dictionary has the last word.

Where do turtles take their cars to get fixed?

To the shell station.

How can circuses afford to hire so many elephants?

Because the elephants work for peanuts.

What's the difference between a piano and a fish?

You can tune a piano, but you can't tuna fish.

What's black and white and makes popping sounds?

A zebra walking on bubble wrap.

What do you call a dog that knows how to tell time?

A watchdog.

Why do bears sleep for six months?

Because nobody dares to wake them up.

What do pigs say in the morning?

Rise and swine!

Why do birds fly south for the winter?

Because they can't drive.

Why do bees have sticky hair?

They use honey combs.

What did one worm say to the other worm?

"Where on earth have you been?"

What do you call a cow in an earthquake?

Milkshake.

What do you call a fish with no eye?

Fsh.

What do you call a pig that knows karate?

A pork chop.

What do you call a cow with no legs?

Ground beef.

What do you say to a nosy bumblebee?

"Mind your own buzz-iness."

What do you call a sad kangaroo?

Unhoppy.

What do you call a kangaroo that gets married?

Hoppily ever after.

What do you call a sleeping dinosaur?

A dino-snore.

What do you say when your bike hits a skunk?

"That stinks."

What did one horse say to the other horse?

"Why the long face?"

What do horses say at bedtime?

"Time to hit the hay."

If there are ten cats in a boat and one jumped out, how many cats would be left?

None, because they're all copycats.

Why was the ant confused?

All of his uncles were ants.

What kind of cookies do birds eat?

Chocolate chirp.

What do spiders eat for Thanksgiving?

Corn on the cobweb.

How do cows celebrate New Year's Eve?

They make moo-year's resolutions.

Why did the whale cross the ocean?

To get to the other tide.

Where do cats go when they lose their tails?

To the retail store.

What do you call a penguin in the desert?

Lost.

What do you call an angry monkey?

Furious George.

Did you hear about the frog whose car ran out of gas?
It had to be toad away.

A man hears a knock on his door and opens it to see a
tiny snail on his welcome mat. He picks up the snail
and throws it as far as he can. One year later, the man
hears another knock on his door. He opens the door
and the little snail is back on his welcome mat. The
snail says, "What was that all about?"

World's Funniest Skeleton Jokes!

What do you call a lazy skeleton?

Lazy bones.

How do you make a skeleton laugh?

Tickle its funny bone.

Why do skeletons make bad liars?

You can see right through them.

What's a skeleton's favorite musical instrument?

The trombone.

What do you call a skeleton detective?

Sherlock Bones.

Why didn't the skeleton go to the dance?

He had no body to dance with.

What do skeletons say when they get angry?

"I have a bone to pick with you."

What do you call a skinny skeleton?

Bony.

How do skeletons open doors?

With a skeleton key.

World's Funniest Invisible Man Jokes!

What did the Invisible Man's wife say when her husband came home late?

"Oh, were you away?"

Why did the Invisible Man turn down a job?

He couldn't see himself doing it.

Why did the Invisible Boy flunk out of school?

His teachers kept marking him absent.

Did you hear about the Invisible Man? He married the Invisible Woman. Their kids are nothing to look at either.

World's Funniest Patient/Doctor Jokes!

Patient: Doc, it hurts when I do this.

Doctor: Don't do that.

Patient: Doc, I tripped on some Legos.

Doctor: Try to block out the pain.

Patient: Doc, I feel crummy.

Doctor: Stop eating cookies.

Patient: Doc, I broke my arm in two places.

Doctor: Don't go to those places.

Patient: Doc, I think I'm turning into a curtain.

Doctor: Pull yourself together.

Patient: Doc, when I wake up in the morning I'm dizzy for an hour.

Doctor: Wake up an hour later.

Patient: Doc, I'm losing my memory.

Doctor: When did this happen?

Patient: When did what happen?

Patient: Doc, will I be able to play the piano after this operation?

Doctor: Of course.

Patient: Good, because I never could before.

Patient: Doc, I think I'm turning into a carrot.

Doctor: Don't get yourself in a stew.

Patient: Doc, I was bitten by a vampire.

Doctor: Drink this glass of water so I can see if your neck leaks.

Patient: Doc, I think I'm insane.

Doctor: I've known that for years.

Nurse: Doctor, there's an invisible man in the waiting room.

Doctor: Tell him I can't see him.

World's Funniest Knock, Knock Jokes!

Knock, knock.

Who's there?

Turnip.

Turnip who?

Turnip the TV, I can't hear it.

Knock, knock.

Who's there?

Isabel.

Isabel who?

Isabel broke, because I thought I heard a knock.

Knock, knock.

Who's there?

Boo.

Boo who?

Why are you crying?

Knock, knock.

Who's there?

Quack.

Quack who?

You quack me up with all these jokes.

Knock, knock.

Who's there?

Lettuce.

Lettuce who?

Lettuce in and you'll find out.

Knock, knock.

Who's there?

Dwayne.

Dwayne who?

Dwayne the bathtub, it's overflowing.

Knock, knock.

Who's there?

Boo.

Boo who?

Why are you crying?

Knock, knock.

Who's there?

Dewey.

Dewey who?

Dewey have to go to school today?

Knock, knock.

Who's there?

Orange.

Orange who?

Orange you going to let me in?

Knock, knock.

Who's there?

Wet.

Wet who?

Wet me in, it's raining.

Knock, knock.

Who's there?

Delight.

Delight who?

Delight is out on de porch.

Knock, knock.

Who's there?

Norma Lee.

Norma Lee who?

Norma Lee I wouldn't knock, but I lost my key.

Knock, knock.

Who's there?

Spell.

Spell who?

W-h-o.

Knock, knock.

Who's there?

Stopwatch.

Stopwatch who?

Stopwatch you're doing and open the door.

Knock, knock.

Who's there?

Mustache.

Mustache who?

I mustache you a question.

Knock, knock.

Who's there?

Wire.

Wire who?

Wire you hiding inside?

Knock, knock.

Who's there?

Olive.

Olive who?

Olive here, but I lost my key.

47

Knock, knock.

Who's there?

Comma.

Comma who?

Comma a little closer and I'll tell you.

Knock, knock.

Who's there?

Harry.

Harry who?

Harry up, I'm waiting for you.

Knock, knock.

Who's there?

Police.

Police who?

Police open the door.

Knock, knock.

Who's there?

Mint.

Mint who?

I mint to tell you something, but I forgot.

Knock, knock.

Who's there?

Harmony.

Harmony who?

Harmony times do I have to knock?

Knock, knock.

Who's there?

Peg.

Peg who?

I peg your pardon, I'm at the wrong house.

Knock, knock.

Who's there?

Sue.

Sue who?

Don't ask me, I'm not a lawyer.

Knock, knock.

Who's there?

Gravy.

Gravy who?

Gravy Crockett.

Knock, knock.

Who's there?

How now.

How now who?

How now, brown cow?

Knock, knock.

Who's there?

Mice.

Mice who?

Mice to meet you?

Knock, knock.

Who's there?

Fishy.

Fishy who?

I find it fishy that you won't open the door.

Knock, knock.

Who's there?

A lonely dog.

A lonely dog who?

A lonely dog who left his bone inside.

Knock, knock.

Who's there?

Luke.

Luke who?

Luke out the window and you'll see. Hee-hee!

Knock, knock.

Who's there?

Thumb.

Thumb who?

Thumb like it hot and thumb like it cold.

Knock, knock.

Who's there?

Tank.

Tank who?

You're welcome.

Knock, knock.

Who's there?

Torch.

Torch who?

Torch you'd never ask.

Knock, knock.

Who's there?

Hair.

Hair who?

Hair today, gone tomorrow.

Knock, knock.

Who's there?

Psst.

Psst who?

Psst, I can see you through the keyhole!

Knock, knock.

Who's there?

Statue.

Statue who?

Statue hiding inside?

Knock, knock.

Who's there?

Easily distracted.

Easily distracted who?

Huh, what did you say?

Knock, knock.

Who's there?

Butter.

Butter who?

Butter bring an umbrella, it's raining.

Knock, knock.

Who's there?

Turn.

Turn who?

Turn around slowly and I'll sneak inside.

Knock, knock.

Who's there?

Waddle.

Waddle who?

Waddle you give if I go away?

Knock, knock.

Who's there?

Sarah.

Sarah who?

Sarah an echo in here?

Knock, knock.

Who's there?

Detail.

Detail who?

Detail is wagging de dog.

Knock, knock.

Who's there?

Ben.

Ben who?

Ben knocking all day for you to open the door.

Knock, knock.

Who's there?

Mikey.

Mikey who?

Mikey is inside, you'll have to open the door.

Knock, knock.

Who's there?

Gladys.

Gladys who?

Gladys you, now let me in.

Knock, knock.

Who's there?

Freddie.

Freddie who?

Freddie or not, here I come!

Knock, knock.

Who's there?

Tori.

Tori who?

Tori to bother you, but I left my key inside.

Knock, knock.

Who's there?

Somebody.

Somebody who?

Somebody who can't reach the doorbell.

Knock, knock.

Who's there?

Will.

Will who?

Will you quit stalling and open the door?

Knock, knock.

Who's there?

Eddie.

Eddie who?

Eddie body home?

Knock, knock.

Who's there?

Lena.

Lean who?

Lean a little closer and I'll tell you.

Knock, knock.

Who's there?

Turkey.

Turkey who?

Gobble, gobble.

Knock, knock.

Who's there?

Don't you dare!

Don't you dare who?

Don't you dare pretend you're not home.

Knock, knock.

Who's there?

Gwen.

Gwen who?

Gwen can we get married?

Knock, knock.

Who's there?

Ida.

Ida who?

Ida be happy if you let me in.

Knock, knock.

Who's there?

Doris.

Doris who?

Doris locked, I can't come in.

Knock, knock.

Who's there?

Wooden.

Wooden who?

Wooden you like to know?

Knock, knock.

Who's there?

Justin.

Justin who?

Justin time for you to let me in.

Knock, knock.

Who's there?

A million dollars!

A millions dollars who?

A million dollars for you if you let me in.

Knock, knock.

Who's there?

Don't ask.

Don't ask who?

I told you not to ask.

Knock, knock.

Who's there?

Snow.

Snow who?

Snow use pretending you're not home, because I know you're in there.

Knock, knock.

Who's there?

Well!

Well who?

Well, if that's how you're going to be, I'll just stay outside!

Knock, knock.

Who's there?

Ken.

Ken who?

Ken I come in?

Knock, knock.

Who's there?

The prettiest girl in the world.

The prettiest girl in the world who?

The prettiest girl in the world who will never speak to you again if you don't open the door.

Knock, knock.

Who's there?

The smartest guy in the world.

The smartest guy in the world who?

The smartest guy in the world, only I forgot my key.

Knock, knock.

Who's there?

Superman.

Superman who?

Superman just flew by and he said for you to let me in.

Knock, knock.

Who's there?

Well I'll be!!

Well I'll be who?

Well I'll be stuck on the porch all day if you don't let me in!

Knock, knock.

Who's there?

Irish.

Irish who?

Irish you a Merry Christmas!

Knock, knock.

Who's there?

Iva.

Iva who?

Iva a kiss for you if you open the door.

Knock, knock.

Who's there?

Nobody.

Nobody who?

World's Funniest Limericks!

Hickory Dickory Dock
I forgot to set my clock.
I'm late for school,
That's really not cool.
I feel like a rusty old sock.

Hippity, hoppity hop,
I fell out of bed with a plop.
I'm late again,
When will it end?
I feel like a raggedy old mop.

Slippery, sloppery slush,
I'm always in such a rush.
Being late is a bummer,
I wish it was summer.
I feel like an old bowl of mush.

It's time for school, I know.
I should be up, but I feel so low.
I've nothing to wear,
My hair is a scare,
So it's back to bed I go.

There's a girl in my class named Jane.
Whose smile is as big as her brain.
She's really quite smart,
With such a big heart,
I'd marry her if I wasn't insane.

I'm hungry so let's go eat.
Something good, but not too sweet.
It's hot outside,
So an orange will tide
My hunger and help beat the heat.

I have a good friend named Zooey,
Who likes to play when it's snowy.
She'll play on her sled
Until she's fed
A lunch of bread and baloney.

I know a young boy named Kyle,
Who runs every day for a while.
He runs so fast,
No one can last
To run with him more than a mile.

There's a girl in my class I like.
The problem's her big brother Spike.
He's big and he's mean,
The toughest I've seen,
He told me to go take a hike.

Not one to be easily swayed,
I told Spike I wasn't afraid.
His face turned all red,
I thought I was dead,
But now he's a new friend I made.

I once knew a boy with no bed,
Who slept upside down on his head
With his feet in the air
And never a care,
It was good for his brain, so he said.

My teacher Miss Rose
Had a wart on her nose.
She had it removed,
Her looks did improve,
But her glasses slid down to her toes.

I once knew a boy from Quebec,
Who was buried in snow to his neck.
When they said, "Are you friz?"
He replied, "Yes, I is—"
"But we don't call this cold in Quebec."

There once was a boy in a tree,
Who was bothered by a big bumble bee.
When they said, "Does it buzz?"
He replied, "Yes, it does."
"It's a regular brute of a bee!"

A tutor who tooted the flute,
Tried to tutor two tutors to toot.
Said the two to the tutor,
"Is it easier to toot?"
"Or to tutor two tooters to toot"

I saw a new dance on TV.
Easy as one, two, three.
But try as I might,
I can't get it right.
A dancer, I'll never be.

I'm in love with a girl in my class.
She loves someone else, so alas,
It's all up in smoke,
My heart is now broke,
I'm glad it's not made out of glass.

At lunch today while eating,
My friend told a joke so fleeting.
A knot in my throat arose,
Milk came out of my nose.
Please don't tell jokes when I'm eating.

A cat once said to a dog,
"You're lazy and you sleep like a log."
Said the dog to the cat,
"At least I'm not fat."
"You eat like a regular hog."

I hope you found this book funny.
I hope your smile is sunny.
Jokes are the best,
They fill you with zest,
Laughter is better than money!

Tips on Telling Jokes

The easiest way to tell a joke is to start with ones that you like. Pick your three favorite jokes out of this book and memorize them. One of the first jokes that I began telling was this one:

If hot and cold had a race, who would win?

Hot would win, because anyone can catch a cold.

I like that joke, because it's funny, it's easy to learn, and it never fails to get a laugh. Speaking of which, don't feel bad if you tell a joke and nobody laughs. Or if the person you told the joke to groans or rolls their eyes. Not everyone has a sharp sense of humor like you and I do. Some people are just naturally unfunny, so don't let it bother you.

Sometimes after you tell a joke, people will ask you for another. So it's good to have two or three jokes up your sleeve at all times; jokes that you like and that are easy for you to memorize.

A good way to approach someone with a joke is to say, "Do you like jokes?" Most people will say yes. Then you can tell them your joke.

Another approach is to say, "I have a joke for you," and then tell your joke.

When telling a story joke, always tell it in the present tense. For instance, don't say, "A boy brought his pet monkey to school. His teacher, who was very mean, said, 'Take that monkey home!' "

Instead, say, "A boy *brings* his pet monkey to school. His teacher, who *is* very mean, *says*, 'Take that monkey home!' "

After you deliver the punch line—the final line of the joke—stop talking. You can smile, but don't laugh at your own jokes.

Of course, the most important part of telling a joke is that it should be fun for you and fun for the person hearing it. Once you start, it's easy. So pick your favorite joke and try it out on someone today!

Other books by Mike Mains

The North Hollywood Detective Club Series

The Case of the Hollywood Art Heist

Teen detectives race to free an innocent man from jail.

When the brother of a classmate is arrested for stealing a valuable painting, Jeffrey Jones and his best friend Pablo Reyes form the North Hollywood Detective Club and set out to rescue him from jail.

The Case of the Dead Man's Treasure

Teen detectives stumble upon the clue to an ancient treasure.

Hired by their teacher to locate a hit-and-run driver, Jeffrey and Pablo find themselves in a race with a ruthless treasure hunter to locate a lost treasure.

The Case of the Christmas Counterfeiters

Two teen detectives. One criminal mastermind. And two billion dollars in counterfeit currency. What could possibly go wrong?

While the rest of the world prepares to celebrate Christmas, Jeffrey and Pablo discover a plot to flood Los Angeles with billions of dollars in counterfeit currency. Their investigation leads them to a criminal mastermind, his hoodlum son, and a mysterious 15-year-old girl who holds the key to the entire puzzle.

The Case of the Deadly Double-Cross

All Jeffrey wanted to do was help a girl at his school find her missing father. He had no way of knowing it would lead to his being arrested for the man's murder.

The Case of the Jilted Juliet

A mysterious note found in a school library book leads Jeffrey and his friends to suspect that a girl who committed suicide thirty years ago might have been murdered.

Monkey Jokes: A Joke Book for Kids!

Tickle your funny bone with these laugh-a-minute jokes for kids. Apes, cheetahs, gorillas, they're all here, ready to entertain you in the world's funniest collection of monkey jokes.

Bodybuilding for Boys & Young Men

If you want muscles and you want them fast, this is the book for you. A fast, fun and effective way to build your body.

Annihilate Your Acne

Do you suffer from acne? Contrary to popular opinion, acne is caused by food allergies and environmental toxins. Eliminate those causes and your acne melts away like a snow cone on a hot summer day. Learn how in this book.

The Impostor Sister Lucy

The true story of Our Lady of Fatima. A must-read book for anyone who wants to go to Heaven.

Heaven. We all want to go there, but very few of us know how. This book explains the necessary steps one must take to achieve eternal salvation. Is anything else in life more important?

Thank you very much for reading this book! If you liked it, please leave a review, because people do read them.

Mike Mains writes mystery, adventure and joke books for young readers.

He loves hearing from readers and can be reached at: mainsmike@yahoo.com